Favorite Wildflowers
Coloring Book

Ilil Arbel

Dover Publications, Inc., *New York*

Favorite Wildflowers Coloring Book is a new work, first published by
Dover Publications, Inc., in 1991.

International Standard Book Number

ISBN-13: 978-0-486-26729-6
ISBN-10: 0-486-26729-6

Manufactured in the United States by RR Donnelley
26729617   2016
www.doverpublications.com

Contents

American Wisteria — 1
Baby-blue-eyes — 2
Bittersweet Nightshade — 3
Bloodroot — 4
Bunchberry — 5
Chicory — 6
Common Wood Sorrel — 7
Common Yarrow — 8
Cow Vetch — 9
Desert Marigold — 10
Downy Lobelia — 11
Farewell to Spring — 12
Few-flowered Shooting Star — 13
Fringed Gentian — 14
Great Globe Thistle — 15
Ivy-leaved Morning Glory — 16
Jewelweed, Spotted Touch-me-not — 17
Jimsonweed, Common Thorn Apple — 18
Large-flowered Trillium — 19
Mayapple — 20
Meadow Rose — 21
Mule-ears — 22

Musk Mallow — 23
Northern Downy Violet — 24
Pennsylvania Smartweed — 25
Pink Lady's Slipper, Moccasin Flower — 26
Pointed Blue-eyed Grass — 27
Round-lobed Hepatica — 28
Sego Lily — 29
Showy Evening Primrose — 30
Showy Orchis — 31
Showy Tick Trefoil — 32
Spring Beauty — 33
Trailing Arbutus, Mayflower — 34
Venus Flytrap — 35
Virginia Strawberry — 36
Water Arum, Wild Calla — 37
Wild Bleeding Heart — 38
Wild Hyacinth — 39
Wintergreen — 40
Yellow Flag — 41
Yellow Rock Nettle — 42
Yellow Skunk Cabbage — 43
Yellow Water Lily — 44

Index of Scientific Names

Achillea millefolium — 8
Baileya multiradiata — 10
Calla palustris — 37
Calochortus nuttallii — 29
Camassia scilloides — 39
Cichorium intybus — 6
Clarkia amoena — 12
Claytonia virginica — 33
Cornus canadensis — 5
Cypripedium acaule — 26
Datura stramonium — 18
Desmodium canadense — 32
Dicentra eximia — 38
Dionaea muscipula — 35
Dodecatheon pulchellum — 13
Echinops sphaerocephalus — 15
Epigaea repens — 34
Eucnide bartonioides — 42
Fragaria virginiana — 36
Gaultheria procumbens — 40
Gentiana crinita — 14
Hepatica americana — 28

Impatiens capensis — 17
Ipomoea hederacea — 16
Iris pseudacorus — 41
Lobelia puberula — 11
Lysichiton americanum — 43
Malva moschata — 23
Nemophila menziesii — 2
Nymphaea mexicana — 44
Oenothera speciosa — 30
Orchis spectabilis — 31
Oxalis montana — 7
Podophyllum peltatum — 20
Polygonum pensylvanicum — 25
Rosa blanda — 21
Sanguinaria canadensis — 4
Sisyrinchium angustifolium — 27
Solanum dulcamara — 3
Trillium grandiflorum — 19
Vicia cracca — 9
Viola fimbriatula — 24
Wisteria frutescens — 1
Wyethia amplexicaulis — 22

Publisher's Note

I N THESE PAGES Ilil Arbel has rendered forty-four of the natural glories of the American landscape. These are flowers that make their homes in swamps, thickets, rock clefts, almost anywhere roots can take hold. Dispersing their seeds through birds and animals and in the wind and water, they may spring up in the most remote and unlikely terrain. Some are rare and delicate, others so hardy as to be weeds. Many are so strikingly beautiful that they have been cultivated, and several have yielded valuable foods and essences. The delight of the hiker, the weekender and the country dweller, the eternal inspiration of art and poetry, the wildflowers exert their gentle allure over the length and breadth of the North American continent.

American Wisteria (*Wisteria frutescens*). Few wild vines can match the beauty of the wisteria in full bloom. It flowers between March and May, and the lilac-colored blossoms hang in long drooping clusters, all but enveloping their host tree. The foliage is first coppery or pink, later dark green; the plant thus stays colorful for a long time. Range: Virginia to Florida, west to Texas.

Baby-blue-eyes (*Nemophila menziesii*). This little flower grows no higher than 12″. The blossoms are bright blue with white centers. They bloom between March and June. Range: Central Oregon to southern California.

Bittersweet Nightshade (*Solanum dulcamara*). A climbing plant, its stem reaches 2–8′ long. Its roots, when eaten, taste first bitter, then sweet. The young green berries later turn bright red; they are poisonous, and the flower was formerly known as Deadly Nightshade. The star-shaped flowers, which appear from May to September, are blue-violet with a yellow central "beak." Range: Nova Scotia to Georgia, west to Kansas and Minnesota.

3

Bloodroot (*Sanguinaria canadensis*). On this small plant, only about 8″ high, each bluish-green leaf enfolds the stem of a single flower. These appear from March to May, and are shining white with yellow stamens. The plant gets its name from the red latex that drips from its stem and roots when broken, which the Indians used as a dye. Range: Nova Scotia to Florida, west to Alabama and Nebraska.

Bunchberry *(Cornus canadensis)*. A creeping plant, rising only 3–8″, with green foliage that turns reddish brown in the fall. The flowers form a yellow-green cluster, surrounded by lighter leaves that look like petals. It blooms from May to July; in the fall the flowers are replaced by clusters of bright-red berries. Range: Newfoundland to Maryland, west to Minnesota and Colorado.

5

Chicory (*Cichorium intybus*). This beautiful and useful plant has the reputation of a weed, being common and easily spread, but it is also widely cultivated. The roots provide the well-known coffee substitute, and the leaves are eaten in salads. It can reach 5′ in height. It has gray-green foliage.

The flowers appear from June to October, and are a light clear blue, or occasionally pink or white. Range: Throughout the U.S. They are a favorite of bees; the Honeybee illustrated here is yellow and black, with yellow-orange pollen baskets on its hind legs.

Common Wood Sorrel (*Oxalis montana*). A small plant, 3–6″ high, found in cool forests. It has delicate light-green sour-tasting leaves, which are eaten in salads. Its flowers, which bloom from May to August, are white with clear purplish stripes. Range: Quebec to Wisconsin and Manitoba, south to North Carolina and Tennessee.

Common Yarrow (*Achillea millefolium*). The yarrow grows to 1–3'. It has gray- or olive-green fernlike foliage, and the flowers in their flat-topped clusters are pink or white with yellowish centers. The plant has been used for medicinal purposes and to make snuff and tea. The flowering period is from June to September. Range: Throughout North America, except the extreme North.

Cow Vetch *(Vicia cracca)*. This vetch is a graceful trailing or climbing plant, growing up to 5′ long. Each of the light-green compound leaves ends in two tendrils. The flowers are violet-blue, but turn pink as they wither. They bloom from May to August in fields and roadsides. Range: Southern Canada, northern U.S.

Desert Marigold (*Baileya multiradiata*). This marigold grows up to 25″ tall and has gray foliage covered with woolly hairs. The flowers, one for each stem, are brilliant yellow. They bloom between April and October. Range: Southern California to Utah and Texas, south to northern Mexico.

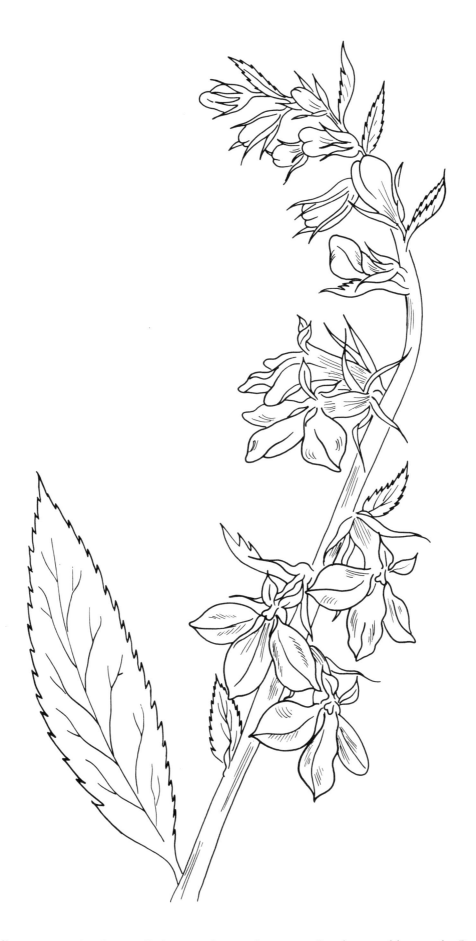

Downy Lobelia (*Lobelia puberula*). A tall plant, reaching up to 4′, with hairy leaves. The flowers, appearing from August to October, are blue-purple. Range: New Jersey west to Kansas and Texas.

Farewell to Spring *(Clarkia amoena)*. The plant grows 1–3′ tall. Its foliage is dark green; the flowers are pink, becoming red-purple in the center, and they bloom from June to August. Range: British Columbia south to California.

Few-flowered Shooting Star *(Dodecatheon pulchellum).* The plant grows up to 20″ tall, the stem rising from a low cluster of leaves. The flowers are unusual: the magenta petals are bent back from a white-and-yellow ring, and the yellow or purple stamens come together into a point below. It blooms from April to July. Range: Coastal prairies west of the Rockies. The Orange Sulphur butterfly *(Colias eurytheme)* is yellow-orange with dark markings; the spots on the hind wings are deep orange.

13

Fringed Gentian *(Gentiana crinita).* A rare and delicate plant, this gentian reaches 1–3½′ in height. The foliage is yellow-green; the beautiful fringed flowers are violet-blue, and they appear late in the year, from August to November. Range: Quebec to Georgia, west to Manitoba and Iowa.

Great Globe Thistle *(Echinops sphaerocephalus)*. A tall plant, up to 7′ in height, with gray-green foliage and tiny blue-gray flowers arranged in globular heads. It is culti- vated for its striking appearance. It blooms from July to October. Range: Quebec to Virginia.

Ivy-leaved Morning Glory *(Ipomoea hederacea)*. A vine, usually 3–6′ long, with twining stems. The delicate funnel-shaped flowers open sky-blue in the morning and turn lavender by evening, when they close and wither. The blooming period is June to October. Range: New England to Florida, west to Texas and North Dakota.

Jewelweed, Spotted Touch-me-not (*Impatiens capensis*). This tall plant grows up to 6'. It has pale-green foliage. The flowers, blooming from July to October, are orange with reddish brown spots. Their shape allows them to be frequently pollinated by hummingbirds. When the seedpods are touched, they spring open and scatter their seeds. The juice from the stems relieves itching from poison ivy and athlete's foot. Range: Newfoundland to Georgia, west to Oklahoma and Saskatchewan. The male Rufous Hummingbird *(Selasphorus rufus)* is mostly red-brown, with an iridescent orange-red throat and bright green on his head and wings.

Jimsonweed, Common Thorn Apple *(Datura stramonium)*. Jimsonweed may grow as high as 5'. Its leaves are dark green; the sweet-scented trumpet-shaped flower is white or purple or both, and its blooming period is June to October. The whole plant is poisonous to both humans and livestock, especially when wilted; merely touching it may cause a rash. Range: Nova Scotia to Florida, west to Texas and Minnesota.

Large-flowered Trillium (*Trillium grandiflorum*). Each stem of this trillium bears three leaves, three sepals and three petals. The large white flower turns pink as it ages. It blooms from April to June in shady woods and thickets, reaching 8–18″ in height; it is also often cultivated. Range: Quebec to Minnesota, south to Georgia and Arkansas.

Mayapple *(Podophyllum peltatum)*. The mayapple grows to 12–18″. Its leaves are dark green on top, lighter underneath. The flower resembles that of the apple. It is white with a yellow center; though large and beautiful, it is often missed because it hangs downward between the two large leaves. It blooms between April and June. The fruit is yellow or brown; it is used to make jelly, though the rest of the plant is somewhat poisonous. Range: Quebec to Florida, west to Texas, Kansas and Minnesota.

Meadow Rose *(Rosa blanda)*. This rose has few or no prickles. It may grow up to 4' high, and its foliage is darker green above than below. The flowers are pink with yellow centers and appear in June and July. Its fruit is the edible red rosehip (shown at lower left), often used for tea and jam. Range: Newfoundland to New Jersey, west to Missouri and Ontario.

Mule-ears *(Wyethia amplexicaulis)*. The plant reaches 2–3′ in height. It gets its name from the shape of its glossy dark-green leaves. The flowers resemble daisies or small sun-flowers; they are bright yellow and bloom from April to June. Range: Washington to Montana, south to Colorado and California.

Musk Mallow *(Malva moschata).* The plant may reach 2' in height. The flowers are white, pink or lavender and have a light musky odor. They bloom from June to September.

Range: Nova Scotia to Virginia, west to British Columbia and Oregon.

Northern Downy Violet *(Viola fimbriatula)*. This tiny flower grows no higher than 4″. The dark-green leaves and stems are covered with soft hairs. The flowers, which bloom in April and May, are violet-purple with white centers. Range: Nova Scotia to Minnesota, south to Louisiana and Oklahoma.

Pennsylvania Smartweed *(Polygonum pensylvanicum).* The plant, which grows to 1–4′ high, has sticky red-green stems. The pink flowers bloom in dense spikes, from June to October. Range: Throughout North America, except extreme North.

Pink Lady's Slipper, Moccasin Flower *(Cypripedium acaule)*. This member of the orchid family grows up to 15″ high. Its foliage is marked with conspicuous veins. The delicate flowers have the familiar slipperlike pink or white lip petal, veined with deeper pink; the sepals around it are greenish brown. It blooms from April to July. Range: Newfoundland to Manitoba and Minnesota, south to South Carolina and Georgia.

Pointed Blue-eyed Grass *(Sisyrinchium angustifolium).* This flower grows to 4–20″ in height. It has grasslike blue-green foliage, and the blossoms are deep blue with yellow centers. The blooming period is from April to July. Range: Newfoundland to Virginia, west to Utah and British Columbia.

Round-lobed Hepatica *(Hepatica americana).* A small plant, 4–6″ high, with rough foliage, this hepatica grows in shady woods. The flowers are blue, purple or white, with green centers and yellow stamens. The Latin name refers to the somewhat liver-shaped leaves, which were once thought to be useful in treating liver ailments. The blooming period is March to June. Range: Nova Scotia to Manitoba, south to Missouri and northern Florida. The insect shown is the bright-red Lady Beetle.

Sego Lily (*Calochortus nuttallii*). This lily may reach a height of 2'. It has gray-green foliage. The flowers are white with a green or lilac tinge; their centers are yellow with purple spots. Their blooming period is May to August. Range: The Dakotas and Nebraska, west and south to New Mexico and California.

Showy Evening Primrose (*Oenothera speciosa*). The plant grows to 8–26" high. Its bright flowers are pink to white, with dark-rose veins and yellow centers. They open in the evening. The flowers bloom from April to July. Range: Missouri to Kansas, south to Texas and Mexico.

Showy Orchis *(Orchis spectabilis)*. A small orchid, 5–12″ in height, with glossy leaves at the base of the stem. The blossoms are purple to pink, with white drooping lips; they bloom from April to June. Range: New Brunswick to Minnesota, south to Georgia and Alabama.

Showy Tick Trefoil (*Desmodium canadense*). A large plant, 2–6′ tall. Its flowers are rose-pink or lavender and appear from July to August. Range: Maine south to South Carolina, west to Missouri and Nebraska.

Spring Beauty *(Claytonia virginica)*. Only 6–12″ tall, with succulent dark-green leaves, this plant has lovely pale-pink flowers with purple veins and a yellow base, which bloom from March to May. Its roots were eaten by the Indians and early settlers. Range: Nova Scotia to Montana, south to Georgia and Texas.

Trailing Arbutus, Mayflower *(Epigaea repens)*. This plant trails along the ground in shady woods for as much as 5'. The flowers, which appear between March and May, are white or pink and very fragrant. Range: Newfoundland to Saskatchewan and Iowa, south to Florida and Alabama.

Venus Flytrap *(Dionaea muscipula)*. This carnivorous plant grows to 4–12″ high. The flowers, which bloom in May and June, are white. The leaves are orange inside and green outside. To obtain nutrients not available from the soil, they trap insects by snapping shut on them after they have been lured in by the leaves' odor. Range: North and South Carolina.

Virginia Strawberry *(Fragaria virginiana).* This most common wild strawberry is a small creeping plant, rising no higher than 8″. The flowers bloom from April to July; they are white with yellow centers. The delicious bright-red berries (which actually appear only after the flower has passed) surpass the cultivated strawberry in flavor. Range: Newfoundland to Florida, west to Alberta and South Dakota.

Water Arum, Wild Calla (*Calla palustris*). This flower grows in bogs and ponds, reaching 6–12″ above water. It has glossy dark-green leaves. Its tiny bright-yellow flowers are arranged on a spike, or spadix, and a large white leaflike spathe surrounds them. Its juice is highly poisonous. It blooms between May and August. Range: Nova Scotia to Hudson Bay, south to Pennsylvania and Iowa. The little Green Frog *(Rana clamitans)* is green or brownish green with dark spots.

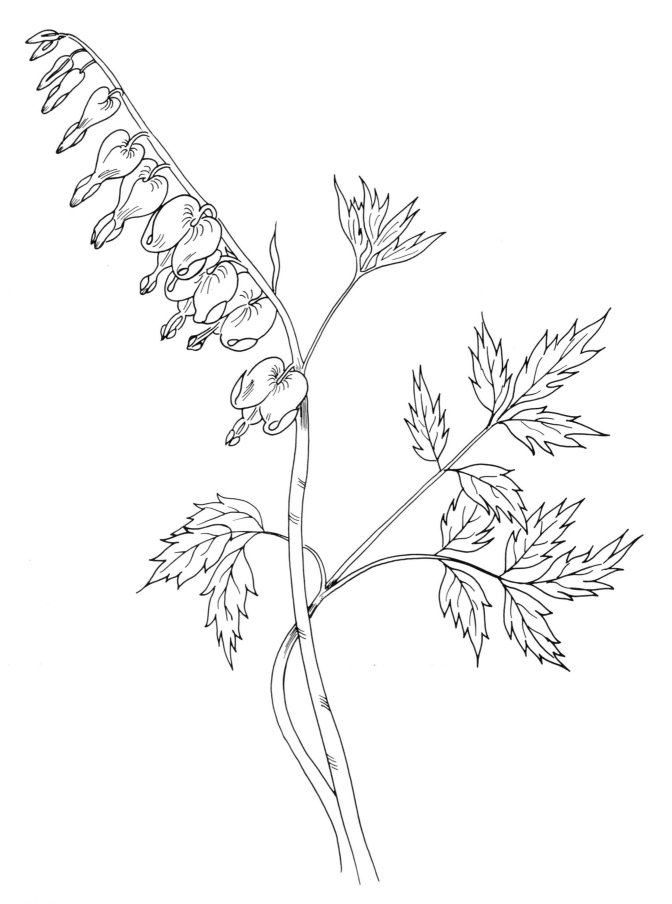

Wild Bleeding Heart (*Dicentra eximia*). The plant grows to 10–20", in rocky terrain. The drooping heart-shaped flowers are pink or red. Varieties of bleeding heart are widely cultivated. Their blooming period is May to October. Range: New York south to Georgia.

Wild Hyacinth *(Camassia scilloides)*. The wild hyacinth grows to 6–24″. It has grasslike foliage, and its flowers are lavender-blue with yellow centers. They bloom from April to June. Range: Pennsylvania and West Virginia, west to Wisconsin and Kansas, south to Georgia and Texas.

Wintergreen (*Gaultheria procumbens*). This small colorful creeping plant grows no higher than 6″. Its evergreen leaves are light-colored when young, darker when mature. The flowers are white, and the "deerberries" that follow (shown on the left in this picture) are cherry-red. The leaves were the original source of oil of wintergreen, used for flavoring and for relieving bodily aches. Range: Newfoundland to Georgia, west to Manitoba and Wisconsin.

Yellow Flag *(Iris pseudacorus)*. This iris may be found in swampy areas. It reaches a height of 2–3′. The flowers, which bloom from May to August, are yellow with dark markings. Range: Newfoundland to Minnesota, south to Georgia and Louisiana. The insect illustrated is a Mayfly; it is light brown with transparent wings.

Yellow Rock Nettle *(Eucnide bartonioides).* A low branched spreading plant. The rough dark-green leaves are covered with stinging hairs. The flowers, which bloom from spring to fall, are bright yellow; they open only in full sun. Range: Texas and Mexico.

Yellow Skunk Cabbage (*Lysichiton americanum*). The plant grows up to 20″, and has light-green foliage. The tiny yellow flowers are arranged on a spike, with a large yellow spathe surrounding them. They bloom between March and June. The flower has a strong and unpleasant odor, which attracts pollinating insects. It is a great favorite of black bears. Range: Northern California and Montana, north to Alaska.

Yellow Water Lily (*Nymphaea mexicana*). The leaves are green, blotched with brown, and usually float on the water. The bright-yellow flower closes at night. It blooms from March to September. Range: South Carolina, Florida, Mexico. The insect is one of the beautiful Damselflies, with its iridescent body and dark transparent wings.